I0426327

MCWP 4-11.1

Health Service Support
Operations

U.S. Marine Corps

To Our Readers

Changes: Readers of this publication are encouraged to submit suggestions and changes that will improve it. Recommendations may be sent directly to Commanding General, Marine Corps Combat Development Command, Doctrine Division (C 42), 3300 Russell Road, Suite 318A, Quantico, VA 22134-5021 or by fax to 703-784-2917 (DSN 278-2917) or by E-mail to **smb@doctrine div@mccdc**. Recommendations should include the following information:

- Location of change
  Publication number and title
  Current page number
  Paragraph number (if applicable)
  Line number
  Figure or table number (if applicable)
- Nature of change
  Add, delete
  Proposed new text, preferably double-spaced and typewritten
- Justification and/or source of change

Additional copies: A printed copy of this publication may be obtained from Marine Corps Logistics Base, Albany, GA 31704-5001, by following the instructions in MCBul 5600, *Marine Corps Doctrinal Publications Status.* An electronic copy may be obtained from the Doctrine Division, MCCDC, world wide web home page which is found at the following universal reference locator: **http://www.doctrine.quantico.usmc.mil**.

Unless otherwise stated, whenever the masculine or feminine gender is used, both men and women are included.

DEPARTMENT OF THE NAVY
Headquarters United States Marine Corps
Washington, D.C. 20380-1775

10 March 1998

FOREWORD

"Corpsman Up!" has echoed across numerous battlefields in America's history. To answer this cry, medical personnel assigned to Marine Corps forces (MARFOR) must be knowledgeable, prepared, and able to provide responsive health service support (HSS) so Marines can do what they do best: win battles. Commanders must be aware of HSS requirements and their contributions to mission accomplishment.

Marine Corps Warfighting Publication (MCWP) 4-11.1, *Health Service Support Operations*, disseminates information on the mission, functions, structure, and concept of employment of HSS units. This publication provides overarching doctrine and establishes a practical approach to HSS from the perspective of the commander or staff officer who can apply it without any significant medical background.

This publication establishes general guidance that requires judgment in application. Lower-level tactics, techniques, and procedures for specific application will be published in MCRP 4-22B, *HSS Field Reference Guide*. This MCWP pertains equally to small-unit leaders and senior commanders.

MCWP 4-11.1 supersedes Fleet Marine Force Manual (FMFM) 4-50, *Health Service Support*, dated 19 September 1990.

Reviewed and approved this date.

BY DIRECTION OF THE COMMANDANT OF THE MARINE CORPS

J. E. RHODES
Lieutenant General, U.S. Marine Corps
Commanding General
Marine Corps Combat Development Command

DISTRIBUTION: 143 000040 00

Health Service Support Operations

Table of Contents

Page

Chapter 8   Patient Movement

Chapter 9   Nuclear, Biological, and Chemical Defense

Chapter 10   Combat Casualty Reporting

Chapter 11   Training

Appendices

Chapter 1

Fundamentals

Focus of health service support (HSS) in the past has been on establishing a large and complex system to maximize returns to duty. Our current focus emphasizes the provision of far-forward, mobile, medical and surgical support and stabilization and rapid evacuation of casualties who are unable to quickly return to duty.

HSS is a process that delivers on demand to the warfighter a healthy, fit, and medically ready force; counters the health threat to the deployed force; and provides critical care and management for combat casualties. Aided by technological innovation and logistics, HSS is the employment of medical forces in support of the warfighter.

HSS supports the National Military Strategy of forward presence and power projection. HSS strengthens the warfighting commander by providing essential care in the theater and rapid aeromedical evacuation (AE) of casualties to enhanced medical treatment facilities in the continental United States (CONUS) for definitive care without sacrificing quality of care.

1001. Mission

The HSS mission is to minimize the effects that wounds, injuries, and disease have on units' effectiveness, readiness, and morale. The mission is accomplished by a preventive medicine program that safeguards personnel against potential health risks and by establishing an HSS system. The system provides support from the point of wounding, injury, or illness and evacuation to a medical treatment facility that can provide the level of care required by the patient.

1002. Principles

HSS principles are guides for planning, organizing, managing, and executing Service support. Seldom will all principles exert equal influence; usually, one or two will dominate a given situation. Identifying which ones have priority is essential to establishing effective HSS. Joint Pub 4-02, *Doctrine for Health Service Support in Joint Operations*, states that each Service component has an HSS system that encompasses—

- Conformity—the medical plan must integrate and comply with the commander's plan.

- Proximity—the medical plan must provide HSS as close to combat operations as the tactical situation permits.

- Flexibility—the medical plan must shift HSS resources to meet changing requirements.

- Mobility—the medical plan must anticipate requirements for rapid movement of HSS units to support combat forces during operations.

- Continuity—the medical plan must provide optimum, uninterrupted care and treatment to the wounded, injured, and sick.

- Coordination—the medical plan must ensure that HSS resources in short supply are efficiently employed and used effectively to support the planned operations.

1003. A Healthy and Fit Force

HSS promotes wellness and ensures quality of life to strengthen the human component of military forces against disease and injury. A healthy force ready to deploy anywhere in the world and ready to withstand hardship and deprivation assures warfighting commanders of physical and mental readiness. Wellness requires continuous attention before, during, and after deployment to sustain maximum readiness and warfighting capability.

1004. Casualty Prevention

HSS focuses on both forms of threat: enemy and health. The enemy threat produces combat casualties, whereas the ever-present threat to health produces disease and nonbattle casualties and is a major source of morbidity throughout military history. The enemy threat depends largely on the enemy's intent to use force and to inflict casualties. The health threat depends on a complex set of environmental and operational factors that combine to produce disease and nonbattle injuries. Failure to counter either threat jeopardizes mission accomplishment and ultimately achievement of the operational objective.

1005. Casualty Care and Management

HSS deploys smaller, mobile, and capable elements to provide essential care in the theater. HSS resources are flexible and adaptable and can be tailored to missions ranging from major theater wars to military operations other than war. The major components of casualty care and management are first response, prehospitalization treatment, forward resuscitative surgery, tailorable hospital care, and enroute care.

1006. Functions

Medical plans must include the following functions into the HSS concept of operations:

- Health maintenance—routine sick call, physical examination, preventive medicine, dental maintenance, record maintenance, and reports submission.
- Casualty collection—selection of and manning of locations where casualties are assembled, triaged, treated, protected from further injury, and evacuated.
- Casualty treatment—triage and treatment (self-aid, buddy aid, and initial resuscitative care).
- Temporary casualty holding—facilities and services to hold sick, wounded, and injured personnel for a limited time, usually not to exceed 72 hours. The medical battalion, force service support group, is the only HSS unit staffed and equipped to provide temporary casualty holding.
- Casualty evacuation—movement and ongoing treatment of the sick, wounded, or injured while in transit to medical treatment facilities. All Marine units have an evacuation capability by ground, air, or sea.

1007. The Hague and Geneva Conventions

The conduct of armed hostilities on land is regulated by the law of land warfare, which is both written and unwritten. The law of land warfare is derived from two principal sources: custom treaties and lawmaking treaties such as the Hague and Geneva Conventions. The rights and duties set forth in these conventions are part of the supreme law of the land. Violation of any convention is a serious offense. Under the Conventions, the signatories established the principle of disinterested aid to all victims of war including those who, through wounds, capture, or shipwreck, are no longer enemies but are merely suffering and defenseless human beings. Additional protocols to the Geneva Conventions, accepted and signed in 1977, established the manner in which the victims of war are to be treated. The Conventions established standards of conduct for medical and religious personnel assigned to aid victims. The United States is a signatory to the Geneva Conventions of 1949 and has directed its military forces to abide by its articles. However, future asymmetrical theaters, especially nonstate actions, may not abide—in fact, probably will *not* abide—by the convention accepted by nation states.

Refer to the following sources for principles of international and domestic law and the status and protection of medical personnel under both Conventions.

- NWP 1-14M/MCWP 5-2.1/COMDTPUB P5800.7, *The Commander's Handbook on the Law of Naval Operations.*

- FM 27-10/FMFM 0-25, *The Law of Land Warfare.*

- DA PAM 27-1, *Treaties Governing Land Warfare.*

(reverse blank)

Chapter 2

Intelligence

Accurate and timely intelligence—knowledge of the enemy and the surrounding environment that is needed to support decision-making—is a prerequisite for military success. Intelligence is a fundamental component of command and control that aids the commander in applying combat power at the decisive time and place. Intelligence activity is mission-focused. In MAGTF intelligence operations, intelligence operations are determined by the commander's intelligence requirements. The resulting intelligence effort provides critical knowledge and understanding about the enemy and the environment to help the commander plan and make decisions.

Medical intelligence includes more than just information on disease or other environmental hazards. Raw data must be analyzed and properly acted on to prevent an adverse operational impact. Medical intelligence from all sources—internal and external to the MAGTF—must be assimilated for the commander to have a complete picture of the medical threat.

2001. Internal Medical Intelligence Sources

Preventive Medicine Section

Most preventive medicine assets organic to the Marine expeditionary force (MEF) are found in the preventive medicine section, headquarters and service (H&S) company, medical battalion, force service support group (FSSG). This section provides general support to all MEF major subordinate commands. General support includes identifying information on environmental health, demographics, living conditions, water supply, waste disposal, insects, diseases, and vector issues of military importance, as well as evaluating local food sanitation and sight and hearing conservation programs.

Local Command G-2 Sections

Additional medical intelligence may be requested through G-2 sections of the command element, ground combat element (GCE), aviation combat element (ACE), and combat service support element (CSSE).

Additional information on intelligence support to medical operations can be found in the intelligence series of the Marine Corps warfighting publications (particularly MCWP 2-3, *Intelligence Analysis and Production*, under development).

Health Service Support Element

The health service support element (HSSE) is often the first to receive medical intelligence from on-site care providers due to multiple communications and information links available to sections within the FSSG combat service support operations center (CSSOC).

2002. The Armed Forces Medical Intelligence Center

The Armed Forces Medical Intelligence Center (AFMIC) is a field production activity of the Defense Intelligence Agency. It is the sole producer of medical intelligence in the Department of Defense (DOD). AFMIC provides all-source intelligence on—

• Worldwide infectious disease and environmental health risks.

• Foreign military and civilian health care systems and infrastructure.

• Foreign biomedical developments and life science technologies of military medical significance.

AFMIC maintains extensive data bases; monitors foreign research, development, production, and transitional flow of medical materiel for military interest; and provides intelligence liaison services to key customers. It also conducts in-house and mobile training, including a medical intelligence fellowship program; serves on numerous intelligence committees and working groups; and trains military reservists for mobilization assignments. AFMIC's intelligence products provide direct support to U.S. military customers for operational planning; development of policy, doctrine, and training priorities; and medical research and development.

Queries for medical intelligence support are addressed via the HSS chain or direct from deploying units to—

Defense Intelligence Agency
Armed Forces Medical Intelligence Center
Fort Detrick
Frederick, MD 21701-5004

or via message to—

DIRAFMIC FTDETRICKMD.

Chapter 3

Operations

The Marine Corps organization for combat is based on its unique assigned force structure. HSS is a mission area common to every MAGTF, regardless of the mission. Definitive operational planning for HSS is always an integral part of all MAGTF operations. The inherent flexibility in the MAGTF and the broad spectrum of potential MAGTF missions call for equal flexibility in HSS execution. The size, type, and configuration of HSS capabilities needed to effectively support a MAGTF will be determined by mission, enemy, terrain and weather, troops and support available-time available (METT-T). The following paragraphs provide an organizational framework for command and staff cognizance within which all HSS operations are executed.

3001. Marine Corps Forces

Marine Corps forces (MARFOR) commanders are responsible for coordinating and integrating HSS within their area of operations. The MARFOR surgeon, dental officer, medical planner, and medical administrative officer advise the MARFOR commander on matters relating to the health of the command, medical logistics, patient movement, sanitation, disease surveillance, medical intelligence, and medical personnel issues, as well as current and future HSS planning at the MARFOR level. Additional duties include serving as the liaison for the commander in chief (CINC) and other component surgeons and monitoring HSS aspects of the time-phased force and deployment data flow.

3002. Marine Expeditionary Forces

MEF commanders are responsible for coordinating and integrating HSS within their area of operations. The MEF surgeon, medical planner, medical administrative officer, preventive medicine officer, hospital corpsmen, and dental technicians are responsible for establishing HSS requirements and ensuring the HSS systems established by MEF major subordinate commands form an integrated and responsive network of support.

The surgeon and the staff also advise the MEF commander on matters relating to the health of the command, medical logistics, patient movement, sanitation, disease surveillance, medical intelligence, medical personnel issues, as well as current and future HSS planning at the MEF level. The MARFOR deals with matters more on the operational level of war, but the MEF is more focused toward the tactical level.

HSS beyond the organic capabilities of the GCE and ACE are normally provided by task-organized units of the medical and dental battalions of the FSSG. Additional support may be needed from designated casualty receiving and treatment ships (CRTSs), fleet hospitals, hospital ships, or medical treatment facilities (MTFs) of other Services.

Marine Division

The medical staff of the division headquarters has a division surgeon, medical planner/administrator, a psychiatrist, and hospital corpsmen. Medical staff responsibilities are similar to the MEF's but are more specifically related to the activities of the GCE. When units smaller than divisions deploy as the GCE, the regiment or battalion surgeons assume much of the planning responsibility associated with health services in addition to their clinical responsibilities. Planning occurs on a company or platoon level, with the hospital corpsmen assisting in the planning.

Marine Aircraft Wing

The medical staff of the Marine aircraft wing (MAW) headquarters has a wing surgeon, medical planner/administrative officer, an environmental health officer, industrial hygienist, optometrist, and hospital corpsmen. Medical staff responsibilities are similar to the MEF's but are more specifically related to the activities of the ACE.

A MAW has four Marine aircraft groups (MAGs). Each MAG has a flight surgeon and several hospital corpsmen. Each MAG is supported by a Marine wing support squadron (MWSS) of the Marine wing support group (MWSG). The MWSS medical staff has a flight surgeon and hospital corpsmen. The flight surgeon is the squadron commander's special staff officer responsible for the aeromedical safety and HSS for the squadron.

Force Service Support Group

The group surgeon advises the commander on the health of the command and the adequacy of internal FSSG HSS. The surgeon also has cognizance over the operation of the group aid station. There is also a health service support officer (HSSO) who coordinates FSSG HSS support for GCE and ACE units requiring medical care that exceeds their organic capabilities. The HSSO serves as the officer in charge of the medical section of the CSSOC during exercises or operations. The FSSG has the majority of the MEF's medical capability. It has a medical battalion with three surgical companies (Surg Co) and eight shock trauma platoons (STPs) to provide initial resuscitative care for casualties.

There is a dental battalion to provide field dentistry when deployed and to advise on dental issues. Medical supplies and equipment for the MEF are managed through the medical logistics company (Med Log Co), supply battalion, which issues the authorized medical allowance list (AMAL) and authorized dental allowance list (ADAL) and handles resupply issues. When the Med Log Co or detachment does not deploy with the CSSE, the CSSE supply detachment and/or inter-Service support agreement provides resupply support.

Medical Battalion

The medical battalion, FSSG is organized to execute HSS functions in support of the MAGTF's mission. The medical battalion provides initial resuscitative HSS support to the MEF and is the only source of organic Marine Corps medical support above the aid station level. Its primary mission is to perform those emergency medical and surgical procedures that, if not performed, could lead to death or loss of limb or body function. The battalion's surgical companies provide initial resuscitative surgical intervention, temporary casualty holding, ground evacuation support to forward medical elements, and preventive medicine support.

The battalion structure has 260 holding beds and 9 operating rooms. The medical battalion is made up of an H&S company and three Surg Co. The H&S company contains 8 STPs that have 10 patient holding beds each. Each Surg Co contains 60 beds and 3 operating rooms.

Surgical Company, Medical Battalion, FSSG. The Surg Co (with support from CSS detachments [CSSDs] to provide power, messing, and transportation) supports regimental-size operations and receives casualties from units or individuals providing first response medical treatment. The Surg Co provides MTFs for resuscitative surgery, medical treatment, and temporary holding of casualties from supported forces. They also prepare and evacuate casualties whose medical requirements exceed the established theater evacuation policy.

The Surg Co is composed of a—

- Headquarters platoon.
- Triage/evacuation platoon.
- Surgical platoon—contains three surgical sections, each supporting an operating room, each operating room capable of staffing two 12-hour shifts.
- Holding platoon—contains 3 ward sections, each containing 20 medical/surgical beds.
- Combat stress platoon.
- Services platoon (ancillary)—services two laboratory sections, two pharmacy sections, and two x-ray sections.

Since the Surg Co is a major link in the chain of evacuation, it should be located, whenever possible, in close proximity to an airfield capable of casualty evacuation by fixed-wing aircraft. Components of the Surg Co may be used to reinforce an STP (i.e., surgical section) to provide a far forward resuscitative surgery capability.

Shock Trauma Platoon, H&S Company, Medical Battalion, FSSG.
The STP is the smallest, most mobile medical support platoon of the medical battalion. It can serve as a beach evacuation station, reinforce a battalion aid station (BAS), operate as an intermediate casualty collecting and clearing point between forward medical elements and the Surg Co, or serve as the forward element of a surgical company (i.e., triage/evacuation platoon) preparing to relocate. An STP reinforced with preventive medicine, group aid station, and dental personnel may also provide HSS to a CSSD or MEU service support group (MSSG).

Dental Battalion

The dental battalion, FSSG provides dental services to the MEF. By attaching task-organized dental sections and detachments to HSSEs of the MAGTF, battalion personnel maintain dental readiness during exercises, deployments, operations other than war, and combat operations.

In an operational environment, the dental battalion's primary mission is to provide dental health maintenance with a focus on emergency care. Personnel from these detachments may also provide postoperative, ward, central sterilization and supply room support, and other medical support as determined to be appropriate by the medical battalion and Surg Co commanders.

The dental battalion commander has additional special staff officer duties as the MEF and FSSG dental officer. As a special staff officer, the dental officer advises the commanders on all professional, administrative, and operational matters in order to optimize use of dental assets.

Medical Logistics Company

The Med Log Co, Supply Battalion, FSSG is a supply operation directly responsible to the FSSG supply battalion commanding officer. The Med Log Co—

- Maintains medical equipment.

- Maintains centralized acquisition, storing, and stock rotation.

- Constructs medical supply sets (AMAL/ADAL).

- Resupplies AMAL/ADAL and line-items in support of HSS units based on specific mission needs.

3003. Marine Expeditionary Unit

Each MEU element deploys with its own organic HSS capability. HSS above this organic level is provided by an HSS detachment (HSSD) task-organized from the medical and dental battalions, FSSG, as part of the MSSG. HSSD structure may include—

- Shock/trauma platoons.

- H&S company, medical battalion elements.

- Med Log Co detachments.

- Dental detachments.

- Surg Co (e.g., triage/evacuation platoons).

The tactical situation ashore will dictate the size of the HSSE capability ashore. This capability may range from a beach or helicopter evacuation station staffed by a triage/evacuation platoon to an STP reinforced with sections of a Surg Co.

3004. Phasing Support Ashore

During the movement phase of amphibious operations, the commander, amphibious task force (CATF) has overall responsibility for HSS services to embarked personnel.

Landing force (LF) HSS personnel aboard ATF ships augment ATF medical and dental departments by providing care to embarked LF personnel using ship's company medical facilities and supplies. LF Class VIIIA equipment and supplies will not be used aboard ship unless authorized by the MAGTF commander in support of an overwhelming emergency.

The senior medical officer of each ATF ship is responsible to the ship's commanding officer for HSS to *all* personnel. If a ship does not have a medical officer, the embarked LF medical officer will have to provide HSS while embarked.

The stages described in the following paragraphs and shown in figure 3-1 represent only notional phasing. Other variations and combinations resulting from such factors as threat level, mission, terrain, geography, weather, force at risk, opposing forces, etc., are possible.

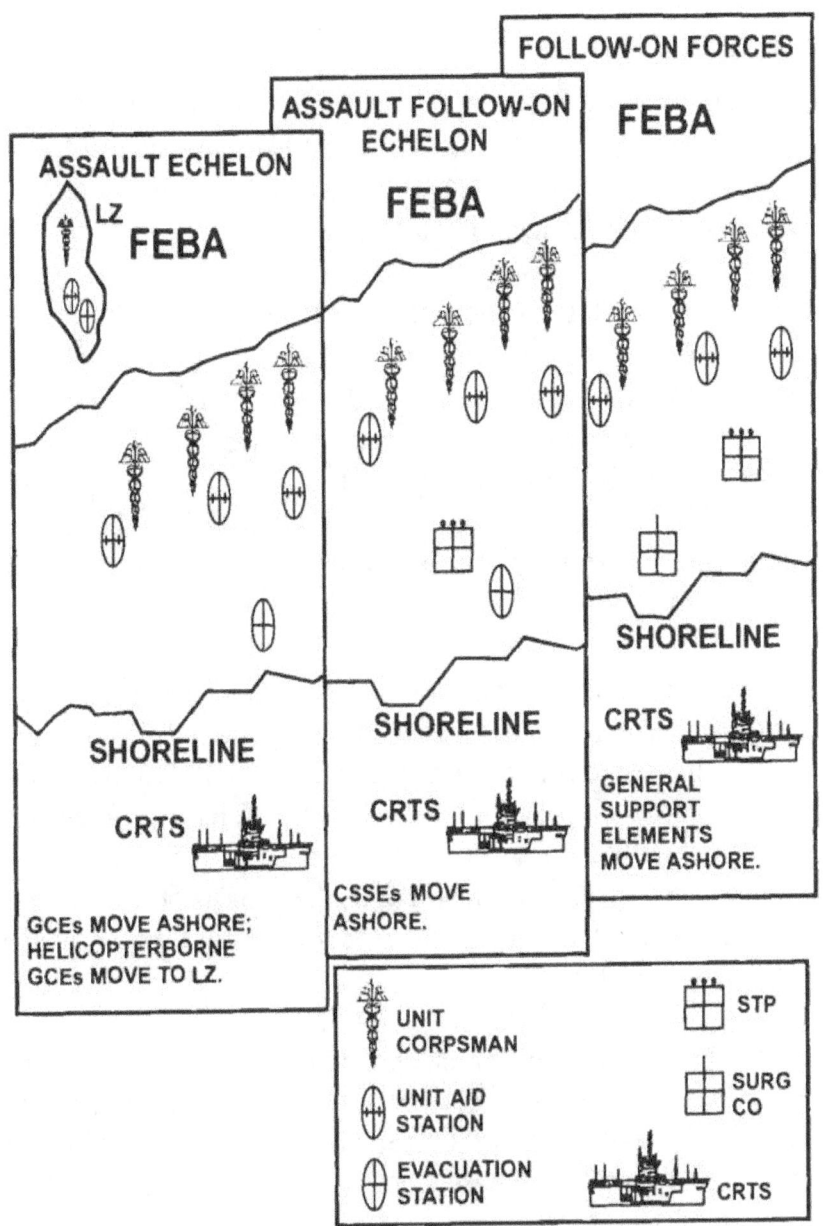

Figure 3-1. Stages of Medical Support in an
Amphibious Operation.

Assault Echelon

During the assault phase, HSS ashore is limited to the capabilities of medical sections organic to combat units. First response medical care for assault forces is provided by self-aid, buddy aid, and corpsmen of landed rifle platoons.

When the tactical situation permits, BASs are established and care from a physician is provided. BASs are normally divided into two sections with assigned battalion nonmedical litter bearers divided between the two sections. One section lands with the battalion combat train and provides in-close support to the assault force. The second section lands with the field train and establishes interim evacuation stations until relieved by follow-on HSSEs.

Evacuation stations are then expanded and staffed by the supporting medical battalion, drawing assets from collection and evacuation sections of STPs or triage/evacuation platoons of surgical companies. When established with the landing force support party (LFSP), the supporting medical battalion constitutes the beach evacuation section(s) of the LFSP. The primary role of a beach evacuation station is to evacuate assault force casualties to designated CRTSs.

When evacuation stations attached to the LFSP become operational ashore, established BASs are relieved to conduct their missions in primary support of parent battalions. Following the landing of supporting evacuation stations, expansion of HSS facilities ashore begins.

Assault Follow-on Echelon

While the majority of CSS capabilities during the AFOE continue to be sea-based, projected HSS capabilities ashore will expand along with the FSSG's. Capabilities could be additional STPs with mobile CSSDs.

When progress of assault units is such that the beachhead is relatively secure, HSS is enhanced from follow-on forces.

Follow-on Forces

HSS shifts its posture to achieve shore-based health care consistent with the expected combat intensity and duration of sustained operations ashore, independent of sea-based facilities. This phasing is achieved by upgrading capabilities ashore by consolidating HSS capabilities ashore with those not yet landed.

If a sustained land campaign is envisioned, additional HSS will normally be provided by fleet hospitals (or other Service equivalent facilities) or hospital ships.

3005. Capabilities External to the MAGTF

Casualty Receiving and Treatment Ships

CRTSs have the largest medical capability of any amphibious ship in the ATF. A CRTS's medical spaces include operating rooms, an intensive care unit, a quiet room, ward beds, and overflow beds. Dental spaces include general dental operating rooms, a maxillofacial surgery operating room, and a prosthetics lab. CRTSs require augmentation by Navy medical department personnel to achieve full casualty treatment capability. Casualties are delivered via helicopter and surface craft. ATF ships suitable for use as CRTSs are the LHD, LHA, and LPH. The CATF's Annex Q, *Planning Guidance, Medical Services*, will designate platforms to serve as CRTSs. For medical support capabilities of these vessels and their potential roles as CRTSs, see Fleet Marine Force Reference Publication 1-18, *Amphibious Ships and Landing Craft Data Book.*

Fleet Hospitals

Fleet hospitals are transportable, medically and surgically intensive, and deployable in a variety of operational scenarios. These HSS assets can be used by theater CINCs, Navy component commanders, and joint task force commanders. Although external support requirements exist, fleet hospitals are substantially self-supporting and relocatable. However, relocatability varies with hospital size. An expedient move would require external transportation equipment. See NWP 4-02.4, *Part A, Deployable Health Service Support Platforms—Fleet Hospitals*, for more information.

Hospital Ships (T-AH)

The T-AH is a floating surgical hospital. Its mission is to provide acute medical care in support of combat operations at sea and ashore. Support may be provided to ATFs, joint task forces, and combined forces. The T-AH is designed to receive patients primarily by helicopter. It has limited capacity for receiving patients by surface craft.

Augmentation

Fleet Surgical Teams. Fleet surgical teams (FSTs) are HSS augmentation teams assigned to the fleet CINCs. Combined, the Pacific and Atlantic fleets have nine teams that are considered the fleet CINC's assets in both peacetime and wartime. FSTs provide medical support to the CINC's routine deployment medical requirements. Medical support for other peacetime contingencies that cannot be covered by the FSTs will be provided by mobile medical augmentation readiness teams (MMARTs).

Mobile Medical Augmentation Readiness Teams. MMARTs provide rapid peacetime response teams of pre-identified medical department personnel trained to augment elements of the operating forces. The Commander Naval Medical Command Instruction 6440.2 series contains a detailed discussion of the MMART.

Medical Augmentation Program. The medical augmentation program (MAP) is the means by which operating forces are brought to wartime manning levels by personnel augmentation from CONUS-based activities. MAP is managed by the U.S. Navy Bureau of Medicine and Surgery (BUMED). In special cases, staffing may be above authorized staffing or in addition to authorized billets when directed by the Chief of Naval Operations. Units participating in MAP include CRTSs, MARFOR HSS units, fleet hospitals, and hospital ships.

(reverse blank)

Chapter 4

Logistics

HSS logistics encompasses the procurement, initial issue, management, resupply, and disposition of material required to support medical and dental elements organic to the MARFOR. Requisitions for Class VIIIA (consumable and equipment) material follow the same channels as other classes of supply. Guidance for planning and procuring Class VIIIB (blood products) is found in DOD Instruction 6480.4, *Armed Services Blood Program Operational Procedures.*

As with all classes of supply, careful consideration should be given to stockage levels of Class VIIIA material. Commanders should not be burdened with moving and maintaining excess material, nor should the need for support ever be delayed because of inadequate access or lack of responsiveness. When the medical planner is developing and planning for appropriate levels of Class VIIIA support, the following information is crucial to ensuring that the entire HSS system is responsive to the commander:

- Concept of operation/scheme of maneuver.

- Combat intensity.

- Duration of the operation.

- Casualty estimates.

4001. Allowance and Source of Logistics

The MAGTF surgeon advises the MAGTF commander regarding medical and dental material support. Allocation of material is documented in the table of equipment (T/E); the AMALs/ADALs; and the normal replenishment supply support. The total T/E and AMALs/ADALs are designed to support a MEF in an estimated worst case scenario for a 60-day period of combat. The quantity of AMALs/ADALs required to support a MEF is determined by the mission requirements of that force. The AMALs/ADALs are to be allocated to support specific requirements. The authorizing commander is responsible for funding AMALs/ADALs above the level prescribed by the Marine Corps order 4400 series.

Table of Equipment

A unit's T/E includes items necessary for basic support of the organization. Examples of this type of equipment include—

- Tentage.
- Vehicles.
- Tools.
- Communications equipment.
- Nuclear, biological, and chemical (NBC) gear.
- Specialized clothing.
- Office equipment.
- Other equipment and supplies, as required.

AMALs and ADALs

AMALs and ADALs are specialized equipment and supply assemblages for medical and dental elements to provide combat HSS. The medical and dental elements have the capability to provide the following services:

- Trauma management.
- Resuscitative surgery.
- Expeditionary laboratory.
- Pharmacy.
- X-ray.
- Dental.
- Preventive medicine.
- NBC treatment.
- Patient holding.
- Sick call.
- Environmental supplements.
- HSS test and repair systems.

See appendix B for a detailed description of AMALs and ADALs.

Normal Replenishment Supply Support

HSSEs deploy with their initial issue and the days of supply prescribed by the MAGTF commander. For the first 60 days of operations, Class VIIIA material beyond this level for the MEF is maintained by the CSSE and provided to supported units as required. For operations more than 60 days, medical resupply is generally provided to the using HSS unit by the CINC's designated single integrated medical logistics manager (SIMLM) via the CSSE.

Single Integrated Medical Logistics Manager

HSS logistics is normally a Service responsibility. However, in joint operations, a SIMLM system may be designated to provide central logistical support to all participating Services in the combatant CINC's area of responsibility. As the dominant user, the U.S. Army has been formally tasked by the DOD to perform the peacetime SIMLM mission in the European and Korean theaters. Under wartime or crisis conditions, the U.S. Army will usually be the dominant Class VIII user and must plan for the SIMLM mission.

The SIMLM system encompasses the provision of medical supplies, medical equipment maintenance and repair, blood management, and optical fabrication to all joint forces within the theater of operations, except Navy combatant ships.

HSS logistics can be provided to Navy hospital ships for common, demand-supported medical supplies in the later stages of theater development. Activation of the SIMLM mission depends on the time-phased force and deployment list supporting the contingency. Air delivery of emergency medical supplies can be used where and when tactically supportable. The CSSE supply detachment, which may include portions of Med Log Co, provides Class VIIIA single-item resupply and, eventually, limited medical repair capabilities to all HSS units of the MAGTF. Supporting combat service support detachments provide medical resupply to medical units of other MAGTF elements.

4002. Individual HSS Equipment

Hospital corpsmen assigned to combat support units of the MAGTF are assigned a complete first aid kit as part of their field gear. These kits may be held by the unit organic supply section and issued on an as needed basis. The corpsmen's parent unit supply section is responsible for ensuring that contents of the first aid kit are maintained in good condition, and that medications have not exceeded their shelf life. Dental officers will be issued a dental instrument and supply set (unit-2).

4003. Routine Resupply

HSS personnel needing resupply will forward requisitions to their unit's supply section. The supply section will, in turn, pass the requisition to the supported activities supply system management unit, or if deployed, the supply section of the CSSE. The CSSE orders, receives, and distributes the required material. While HSS personnel may be of help in identifying alternate doses or approved substitutes, care is required in using alternate sources of supply, other than those already approved by the Defense Medical Standardization Board or Navy Medical Logistics Command. HSS personnel may also assist in identifying the location of other U.S. medical facilities where required items may be obtained.

4004. Combat Resupply

During embarkation planning, HSS planners determine the number and type of AMALs/ADALs required to support the assault phase of the operation. Additional Class VIIIA consumable material will be positioned for deployment with the supply section of the CSSE. After the consumable AMALs/ADALs modules are issued and expended, or when directed, resupply will be accomplished by normal line item requisition from the supporting CSSE. When stockpiles of MAGTF Class VIIIA are expended, Class VIIIA will be obtained through the designated SIMLM provider.

4005. Patient Movement Items

Patient movement items (PMI) are the medical equipment and supplies required to support the patient during evacuation, e.g., ventilators, vital sign monitors, and blankets. Handling and return of equipment to the aeromedical evacuation (AE) system requires a reliable supporting logistics infrastructure to ensure that PMI are available and serviceable. The plan for a PMI exchange system and the return of AE equipment and PMI to the originating MTF should be addressed in the respective operation plan (OPLAN).

When a patient requires evacuation, the originating MTF has responsibility to provide the PMI. These items accompany a patient throughout the chain of evacuation from originating MTF to destination MTF, whether it is an intra- or intertheater transfer.

The Services will include and maintain initial quantities of PMI in the appropriate medical assemblages.

4006. Disposal of Materials

Disposal of soiled, contaminated, or other unserviceable Class VIIIA items must be accomplished with due consideration for the safety of U.S. forces and local civilian populations.

Disposal must also be in compliance with local and international laws, ordinances, or customs governing such disposal whenever operations allow. When disposal takes place in the U.S. or its territories, Class VIIIA disposal is coordinated with the local office of the Defense Reutilization Marketing Office. Peacetime disposal overseas is coordinated under the guidance of the Defense Reutilization Marketing Office or supporting CSSE.

When the tactical situation permits during combat operations, the safest method of field disposal is burning, followed by deep burial (over 6 feet). The burial site must be located at a safe distance from watersheds and populated areas. Responsibility for neutralization and disposal of clothing, equipment, and dressings removed during NBC decontamination processes resides with the command's NBC officer.

Disposal of body parts, tissues, and Class VIIIB blood and blood products obtained during operative or diagnostic procedures is, preferably, accomplished in the same manner as used by local medical facilities. Alternative disposal by burning or deep burial requires prior authorization and specific guidance of higher authority. Prior coordination with local health authorities and religious leaders should be accomplished whenever possible.

4007. Protection of Medical Supplies

Medical material and supplies are protected under the law of land warfare and the Geneva Conventions. However, when medical material and supplies are mixed with combat supplies, they lose the protection afforded by these covenants. Marking of medical material and supply storage areas with the red cross of the Geneva Conventions is a tactical decision to be made by the area commander. The Geneva Conventions and the law of land warfare prohibit the destruction of medical material and supplies that must be abandoned in a retrograde movement occasioned by enemy action or other tactical considerations.

Chapter 5

Planning

HSS planning occurs at all levels of command and organizations across the range of military operations. All commanders are responsible for the health and welfare of their troops. All commanders have HSS staffs that plan from the strategic level of war through the tactical level of war.

5001. Joint Guidance

Chairman of the Joint Chiefs of Staff Manual (CJCSM) 3122.03, *Joint Operation Planning and Execution System, Volume II, Planning Formats and Guidance,* sets forth administrative instructions and formats to develop OPLANs of combatant commands, subunified commands, joint task forces, and their subordinate component commands. It may also be applied when significant forces of one Service are attached to forces of another Service.

OPLANs, concept plans (CONPLANs), functional plans, and operation orders (OPORDs) prepared by commanders to fulfill tasks assigned in the joint strategic capabilities plan (or otherwise directed by the Chairman of the Joint Chiefs of Staff) will conform to the guidance contained in CJCSM 3122.03. To facilitate communications on operation planning among military headquarters, commanders will standardize the format and content of other appropriate plans according to CJCSM 3122.03.

5002. Annex Q, Planning Guidance, Medical Services

Guidance for medical services is located in Annex Q, *Planning Guidance, Medical Services*, of OPLANs, CONPLANs, functional plans, and OPORDs. Annex Q identifies requirements and provides guidance to subordinate commanders and their HSS planners. The following are sample HSS appendices to Annex Q:

- Appendix 2, Joint Blood Program.

- Appendix 3, Hospitalization.

- Appendix 4, Patient Movement.

- Appendix 6, Medical Logistics (Class 8A) System.

- Appendix 7, Preventive Medicine.

- Appendix 8, Medical Command, Control, and Communications.

Chapter 6

Command and Control

Command and control (C^2) for HSS is the combination of HSS organizations, people, communications systems, architecture, and medical information which provides the commander timely information to make decisions. C^2 for HSS entails all functions necessary for medical units to rapidly execute HSS functions in response to the needs of the supported unit.

There are four major C^2 areas:

- C^2 organization.

- Communications and information systems.

- Information management.

- MAGTF C^2 centers, agencies, and facilities.

In combination these areas develop, process, and disseminate orders and information to subordinate units and provide the means to receive and implement orders from a higher authority. All of these areas interact to produce effective and harmonious actions.

6001. C^2 Organization

HSS is a part of every level of the MAGTF. Communications assets available vary. HSS shares these assets with other warfighting functions. In the Marine Corps, the same radios that carry fire support or command information will also carry medical information. The same telephones and switches that commanders use are also used by HSS personnel. There is no "separate" or "dedicated" medical network in the tactical Marine Corps communications architecture. Rather, the architecture supports "common users" who share its resources.

Units responsible for providing detachments which support C^2 for HSS operate under the staff cognizance of the G-6/S-6 (communications and information systems officer) of the supported unit. Marines assigned to these units, in concert with the personnel assigned to the G-6/S-6 sections and HSS organizations, ensure that an effective communications and information systems (CIS) network is planned, installed, operated, and maintained.

6002. Communications and Information Systems

CIS provide management and decision support tools for the HSS commander and staff to collect, transport, process, disseminate, and protect voice, data, and information.

CIS include tactical single channel VHF, SHF, HF, and UHF radios; tactical and commercial telephones; multichannel digital systems; satellite communications; cryptographic equipment; and data systems for classified and unclassified local area network/wide area network (LAN/WAN) connectivity. All of these systems are used by common units and are allocated in accordance with the commander's priorities.

To improve interoperability, increase efficiency, and reduce costs, DOD has mandated that the Services move to a common set of information systems and services. This implementation is occurring with the fielding of the Global Command and Control System (GCCS) and the implementation of the defense information infrastructure (DII) common operating environment (COE).

HSS uses the Joint Operation Planning and Execution System (JOPES) for planning and execution under GCCS. JOPES combines joint policies, procedures, personnel, training, and a reporting structure supported by automated data processing on GCCS. The medical analysis tool (MAT) is the HSS requirements generator and analysis tool supported by GCCS at the Marine Corps component level for planning and execution of HSS.

MEF

CIS support for HSS organizations will be provided by communications battalion. The G-6/S-6 must plan for connectivity among the division, wing, and FSSG as well as external communications with organizations in the joint arena.

Division

CIS support for HSS personnel will be provided by communications company, H&S battalion.

Wing

CIS support for HSS personnel will be provided by the Marine Wing Communications Squadron (MWCS) and Marine Wing Support Group (MWSG).

FSSG

CIS support for HSS personnel will be provided by communications company, H&S battalion and communications platoon, medical battalion.

Deployed MEF

CIS support for HSS personnel will come from both the Navy CIS system and communications battalion.

6003. Information Management

HSS has traditionally been supported by a variety of information systems and procedures that aided the user in the collection, analysis, presentation, and storage of information. Systems used unique hardware and software configurations that performed specialized functions. These systems typically were unable to access or share data and information with other systems. New designs have been developed that consolidate as well as improve accessing and sharing information. This migration has continued under the auspices of the Theater Medical Information Program (TMIP).

TMIP's mission is to provide integrated automation of the theater medical environment. TMIP provides a global capability linking HSS information data bases and integration centers that are accessible to the warfighter while engaged in any mission. The link is essential to aid theater commanders to make time-sensitive decisions critical to the success of their operations. The link is accomplished by integrating the GCCS with the Global Combat Support System. TMIP integrates HSS capabilities under a joint concept of operations to assist the HSS commander/theater surgeon and to support the delivery of responsive combat medical care. TMIP establishes the means to combine existing, developing, and future medical information.

TMIP's C^2 capabilities collect medical information about personnel, medical units, facilities, equipment, supplies, and training during alert/mobilization, deployment/sustainment, and reconstitution/redeployment. Information is received, processed, displayed, and analyzed to generate and publish plans and orders. TMIP enables the assessment of personnel medical status and the readiness and capabilities of the HSS units. The program provides the required information links to HSS organizations and enables rapid decisionmaking on—

- Medical capabilities assessment and sustainability analysis.
- Medical threat/intelligence.
- Combat casualty care.
- Medical logistics.
- Blood management.
- Patient movement.
- Manpower/training.

6004. MAGTF C^2 Centers, Agencies, and Facilities

The main MAGTF C^2 center, agency, or facility for HSS will be found in the combat service support operations center (CSSOC) of the FSSG. The CSSOC is the agency within the CSSE and subordinate CSS units that controls and coordinates the day-to-day operations of the CSS organization. At the FSSG, the CSSOC is operated by the G-3/S-3. Within the ACE, these duties are performed by the G-4/S-4 at the MWSG/MALS/MWSS levels.

The CSSOC's are centrally organized around the functional areas of supply, health services, maintenance, engineer, transportation, and services. The CSSOC controls the CSS radio nets and has direct telephone lines to subordinate units, supported units, and higher headquarters.

Chapter 7

Preventive Medicine

Disease and nonbattle injuries can have a rapid and widespread impact on the effectiveness of our military organizations. The devastation of disease and environmental hazards on personnel is not isolated to the people of a Third World developing nation. Throughout history, military forces have lost more personnel to disease and nonbattle injuries than to wounds sustained in combat. During the Civil War, more Federal soldiers died from disease than wounds. Approximately 44,238 were killed in battle; 49,205 died of wounds; and 186,216 died of disease.

Preventive medicine efforts can dramatically reduce the incidence of disease during military operations. Proactive preventive medicine measures should be incorporated into all levels of care. Real-time disease surveillance data should be used to brief commanders on potential medical and environmental threats and on the effectiveness of preventive medicine measures.

Prevention of disease and nonbattle injuries is a critical function of the HSSE. Naval Medical (NAVMED) P-5010, *BUMED Manual of Naval Preventive Medicine*, prescribes specific preventive medicine measures.

7001. Pre-Deployment

Specific preventive medicine taskings and efforts to be conducted before deployment include—

- Collecting and disseminating environmental and epidemiological information on the theater of operations to the supported commander, HSS units, and MAGTF elements that might be affected, for use in planning and action as changes occur.

- Recommending personnel augmentation requirements to support the OPLAN.

- Recommending immunizations and other preventive measures to counter medical threats within the theater of operations and in-transit staging points.

- Training individuals (through unit training) in personal hygiene, personal protective measures, protection equipment, and field sanitation practices.

- Assisting medical units in completing pre-deployment requirements (immunization, preventive medicine threat briefings, and permethrin treatment of clothing) and in preparing for embarkation of preventive medicine equipment.

7002. Deployment

Specific preventive medicine taskings and efforts to be conducted while deployed include—

- Disseminating militarily significant preventive medicine information to commanders and HSS units in the theater of operation.

- Providing technical oversight on food service operations and procurement.

- Providing oversight and testing at water points and bulk water storage areas.

- Conducting disease vector and pest surveillance and control when feasible.

- Maintaining environmental health and pest control equipment.

- Conducting weekly disease and injury surveillance at all battalions and squadrons.

7003. Marine Expeditionary Force Preventive Medicine Sources

The MEF surgeon's staff includes a physician (the preventive medicine officer) with special expertise in preventive medicine and public health. This physician is responsible to the MEF commander and MEF surgeon for coordinating preventive medicine efforts among the division, the wing, and the FSSG.

Most preventive medicine assets organic to the MEF are found in the FSSG's preventive medicine section of the medical battalions' H&S company. The section is responsible for providing general support to all MEF commands. Support includes identifying information regarding environmental health factors; demographics; living conditions; water supply; waste disposal; insects; diseases and vector issues of military importance, and evaluating local food sanitation, sight, and hearing conservation programs.

7004. Mobile Medical Augmentation Readiness Team

During peacetime, any operational commander may request preventive medicine MMART assistance from the Chief of Naval Operations (N931) via the operational chain of command.

7005. Navy Environmental Health Center

The Navy Environmental Health Center, located in Norfolk, VA, supports operational units. It conducts—

- Risk screening.
- Data evaluation.
- Exposure assessments.
- Toxicity assessments.
- Health risk evaluations.
- Health and safety planning.
- Environmental risk communication workshops and seminars.

The Navy Environmental Health Center and its supporting activities establish and disseminate preventive medicine and environmental protection policy recommendations for BUMED. Field activities in direct support of the Center follow:

- Navy Environmental Preventive Medicine Units—provide updated disease information on areas of the world or specific countries, public health and preventive medicine issues, and occupational health and safety support to military forces.

- Navy Disease Vector Ecology and Control Centers—provide technical and specialized services in the field of disease vector surveillance and control, as well as providing vector control training to various agencies of the federal government. These centers test and evaluate vector control equipment and techniques, collect, summarize, and disseminate disease vector and health threat information. This diverse mission includes a special emphasis on contingency response in the event of armed conflicts, military operations other than war, and operational support of both fleet and shore activities.

- Forward Deployed Laboratory—can quickly identify infectious and biologic threats to the deployed force. During contingency operations, the task force commander may request the support of this deployable, advanced public health laboratory (NWP 4-02, *Operational Health Service Support*).

7006. Additional Resources

The Naval Medical Research and Development Command conducts basic clinical and applied field research directly related to military requirements and operational needs. It is located in Bethesda, MD.

The Naval Medical Research Institute provides research related to immediate operational problems, which include heat stress research that leads to exposure limits for hot-humid shipboard environments; safety equipment, including protective clothing, flight goggles, safety belts, and repellents for insect vectors of disease and sharks. It is also located in Bethesda, MD.

(reverse blank)

Chapter 8

Patient Movement

Patient movement is a casualty management system. It is designed to coordinate the movement of casualties from site of injury or onset of disease through successive levels of care to a facility that can provide the appropriate level of treatment. Prompt movement of casualties through the evacuation system to treatment facilities is essential to decrease morbidity and mortality of battlefield casualties. If casualties occurred at regular intervals, in constant numbers, at predetermined locations, and with predictable injuries, their movement would require little or no coordination. Patient movement is a vital support factor that must be planned. Personnel must be trained on equipment and procedures in advance of operations in the field.

8001. Phases

Coordination of casualty movement is especially critical during operations when casualties must be moved from shore to task force ships. When properly followed, the medical regulating process ensures that patients move only as far rearward in the continuum of care as their health needs dictate which, in turn, assures the efficient and effective use of the limited HSS assets available to the MAGTF. Patient movement may occur in two phases:

Evacuation—the movement of patients between point of injury or onset of disease to a facility that can provide the necessary treatment capability.

Medical regulating—the process of selecting destination MTFs with the necessary HSS capabilities for patients being medically evacuated in, between, into, and out of different theaters of geographic combatant commands and CONUS.

8002. Decisionmaking

Degree of care for the sick and wounded in any area of combat is greatly influenced by prevailing tactical situations. Conditions are seldom static, and success in combat must remain the primary goal of combat, combat support, and combat service support units. This environment requires a dynamic casualty management decisionmaking process which must be applied at all HSS units and in the patient movement system.

Casualty Sorting (Triage)

An effective process of casualty sorting, also referred to as triage, is basic to the successful operation of a patient movement system. Rapid evaluations must be made to identify which patients need immediate resuscitation and which patients can tolerate delay in treatment. Deciding which patients should be moved after initial treatment to other medical facilities is of equal importance.

Medical Management

Under combat conditions, the flow of sick and wounded puts variable pressure on capabilities of medical facilities. Incoming casualties necessitate the movement of stable casualties who can be evacuated. Close coordination between clinical and administrative services must be maintained to achieve effective management of individual casualties. Medical officers who are responsible for decisions on movement of individual casualties must work closely with administrative officers charged with implementing patient movement for evacuation. Underlying all considerations is the basic objective of preserving life and limb.

8003. Medical Evacuation Assets

The assigned mission dictates the number and types of aircraft assigned to accomplish all assault support tasks. This mission, along with the limited number of aircraft in the Marine Corps inventory, precludes the assignment of dedicated aeromedical evacuation (AE) aircraft in most cases. All Marine Corps rotary wing transport and utility aircraft have the capability to perform an AE mission. Allocation of aircraft to perform the AE mission would be at the discretion of the MAGTF commander. Assets are designated to perform AE through implied mission tasking or by assuming a standby posture.

Prior planning is essential to ensure proper allocation of aircraft to support AE missions. Within the MEF, the FSSG HSSE, in conjunction with the FSSG logistics movement coordination center (LMCC), plans for medical evacuation aircraft. The LMCC air liaison officer is the direct link to the MAW for identification of medical evacuation missions in the air tasking order. In the absence of an AE capability, casualty evacuation is accomplished using any surface (water or ground) transportation available (ground ambulance, five-ton truck, small boat, landing craft air cushion).

Evacuation concepts used by the Marine Corps are defined as the following:

Dedicated medical evacuation assets are patient movement assets configured for medical evacuation, externally marked with a red cross, and specifically reserved to support the medical evacuation mission. Dedicated medical evacuation assets are authorized protection under the Geneva Conventions.

Designated medical evacuation assets are nonmedical patient movement assets, not externally marked with a red cross, but configured and allocated for patient movement. Designated medical evacuation assets are not afforded protection under the Geneva Conventions.

8004. Aeromedical Evacuation Request Procedures

Normally, when control is seabased, units request AE by radio to the helicopter direction center using the helicopter direction net. When command and/or net control has been passed ashore, units request AE from the direct air support center using the tactical air request/helicopter request net. The air officer will then consult with either the ATF medical regulating control officer when seabased or the LF patient evacuation officer when ashore for a recommendation of the best medical facility to care for the patient.

In operations where dedicated AE assets are assigned, the direct air support center will make liaison with the units responsible to provide AE.

AE missions are classified as preplanned or immediate. Both types of support are delivered in response to specific requests via the assault support request.

AE missions from Marine Corps MTFs to theater hospitals will be coordinated by the patient evacuation/patient movement section, FSSG, in coordination with the HSSE, the CSSOC, LMCC, and the theater patient movement requirements center.

8005. Further Guidance

NWP 4-02.2 Vol. 1, *Patient Movement*, provides a general summary of the HSS system and the specific tactic, techniques, and procedures (TTP) for naval expeditionary force medical regulating. For joint operations, refer to Joint Pub 4-02.2, *Joint Tactics, Techniques, and Procedures for Patient Movement in Joint Operations*.

(reverse blank)

Chapter 9

Nuclear, Biological, and Chemical Defense

All military personnel must be prepared to operate in a contaminated environment. HSS personnel must also be prepared to provide patient care in an NBC environment. Decontamination of patients and transportation assets causes evacuation delays, making first aid and patient care even more critical. Since the staffing of HSS units is based on conventional warfare requirements, these units will be taxed in their ability to provide effective HSS.

NBC actions cause high casualty rates, materiel losses, obstacles to maneuver, and contamination. Mission-oriented protective posture (MOPP) levels 3 and 4 result in body heat buildup, reduced mobility, and degraded visual, touch, and hearing senses, ultimately reducing unit effectiveness.

Contamination is a major problem in providing HSS in an NBC environment. To maximize the unit's survival and effectiveness, commanders must take action to avoid NBC contamination by making maximum use of alarm and detection equipment and unit dispersion; overhead shelters, shielding materials, and protective covers; collective protection shelters; and chemical agent resistant coatings.

On a contaminated battlefield, the focus is on keeping the Marine in the battle. Effective and efficient triage, emergency treatment, decontamination, and contamination control in the operational area save lives, assure prompt evacuation, and maximize the return-to-duty rate.

9001. Before a Nuclear, Biological, or Chemical Attack

Before an NBC attack, HSS personnel must train to survive the attack, to operate the MTF in the environment, and to effectively care for NBC casualties. HSS personnel must keep their immunizations current, use available preventive treatment against suspected agents, pretreat for suspected agents, and have antidotes and essential Class VIIIA supplies readily available for known or suspected chemical or biological agents.

The best defense for HSS personnel is to protect themselves, their patients, Class VIIIA supplies, and equipment by following contamination avoidance procedures. HSS personnel must ensure that stored Class VIIIA supplies and equipment are in protected areas or in their storage containers with covers in place.

One method of protecting supplies and equipment is to keep them in their shipping containers until needed. When time permits after receiving warnings that an NBC attack is imminent or that a downwind hazard exists, HSS personnel should seek protected areas such as basements, culverts, and ravines for themselves and their patients.

9002. During a Nuclear, Biological, or Chemical Attack

HSS personnel and their patients should remain in the best available protected areas and take up positions within the shelter that are away from windows and other openings. They move out of these positions only when notified that it is safe to do so. In the absence of higher authority, HSS personnel use caution in their movements.

9003. After a Nuclear, Biological, or Chemical Attack

HSS personnel must survey their equipment to determine the extent of damage and their capabilities to continue the mission. Initially, patients from nuclear detonations will be suffering thermal burns or blast injuries. Also, HSS personnel may expect disorientation in patients and other HSS personnel.

Normally, radiation-induced injuries are observed within a few hours or days of the attack. Chemical agent patients manifest their injuries immediately upon exposure to the agent. However, blister agent patients can show signs of exposure immediately or up to 14 days later. Biological agent patients may not show any signs of illness for hours to days after exposure.

All patients receiving treatment must be checked for NBC contamination. Patients are decontaminated before treatment to reduce the hazard to HSS personnel, unless life- or limb-threatening conditions exist. Patients requiring treatment before decontamination are treated in the HSS area of the decontamination station. Cardiac arrest, massive hemorrhage, and respiratory distress are conditions that may require treatment in the decontamination area.

9004. Nuclear Environment

The HSS unit must continue its support mission in a nuclear environment by preparing protective shelters. Well-constructed foxholes with overhead cover and expedient shelters (reinforced concrete structures, basements, railroad tunnels, or trenches) provide good protection from nuclear attacks. Armored vehicles also provide protection against both the blast and radiation effects of nuclear weapons. Casualties generated in a nuclear attack will likely suffer multiple injuries (combinations of blast, thermal, and radiation injuries) which complicate HSS. Nuclear radiation casualties fall into three categories.

The irradiated casualty has been exposed to ionizing radiation but is not contaminated. These casualties are not radioactive and pose no radiation threat to medical care providers. Casualties who have suffered exposure to initial nuclear radiation fit into this category.

The externally contaminated casualty has radioactive dust and debris on clothing, skin, or hair. This presents a "housekeeping" problem to the MTF similar to the lice-infested patient arriving at a peacetime MTF. However, this contamination may present a threat to HSS personnel. The externally contaminated casualty is decontaminated at the earliest time consistent with required medical care. Lifesaving care is always rendered before decontamination.

The internally contaminated casualty has ingested or inhaled radioactive materials, or radioactive material has entered the body through an open wound. The radioactive material continues to irradiate the casualty internally until radioactive decay and biological elimination removes the radioactive isotope. Attending HSS personnel are shielded, to some degree, by the patient's body. Inhalation, ingestion, or injection of quantities of radioactive material sufficient to present a threat to medical care providers is highly unlikely.

9005. Biological Environment

A biological attack may be difficult to recognize because frequently it does not have an immediate affect on exposed personnel. HSS personnel must monitor for biological warfare indicators such as—

- An increase in disease incidences or fatality rates.

- A sudden presentation of an exotic disease.

- Other sequential epidemiological events, especially when presented in lines of communications.

Passive defensive measures (such as immunizations, good personal hygiene, physical conditioning, use of arthropod repellents, use of protective mask, and practice of good sanitation) lessen the effects of most biological intrusions.

Commanders of MTFs must enforce contamination control to prevent injury to HSS personnel and to preserve the MTF's integrity. Incoming patients and equipment must be surveyed for contamination. Ventilation systems in medical treatment facilities without collective protection shelters must be turned off if biological or chemical exposure is imminent.

Decontamination of most biologically contaminated patients and equipment can be accomplished with soap and water.

Patients exposed to a biological agent may require observation and evaluation to determine necessary medications, isolation, or treatment.

9006. Chemical Environment

Handling chemically contaminated patients presents a great challenge to HSS units. The vapor hazard associated with contaminated patients may require HSS personnel to remain at MOPP level 4 for long periods; therefore, HSS personnel must locate clean areas to set up their MTF. The MTF should operate in a contaminated environment only until HSS personnel have the time and means to move to a clean area.

9007. Medical Evacuation

An NBC environment forces the unit commander to consider what evacuation assets will be committed to the contaminated area. If operating forces are in a contaminated area, most or all of the medical evacuation assets will operate there. However, efforts should be made to keep some ambulances free of contamination.

There are three basic modes of evacuating casualties: personnel, ground vehicles, and aircraft. Commanders must recognize the constraints NBC warfare places on casualty evacuation during operations and then plan and train to overcome these deficiencies.

9008. Personnel Considerations

Medical treatment requirements increase when operating in an NBC contaminated environment. As a result, HSS personnel reinforcement and replacement may be necessary. Plans for HSS following an NBC attack must include efforts to conserve available HSS personnel and ensure their best use. HSS personnel provide emergency medical treatment or advanced trauma management and more definitive treatment as time and resources permit. However, to provide definitive care, they must be able to work in a shirt-sleeved environment, not in MOPP levels 3 or 4. Non-HSS personnel conduct search and rescue operations for the injured or wounded; they also provide immediate first aid and decontamination.

(reverse blank)

Chapter 10

Combat Casualty Reporting

Commanders must be thoroughly familiar with combat casualty reporting procedures. The G-1/S-1 section of a command is responsible for submitting prompt, accurate, and complete casualty reports to higher headquarters. In combat operations, unit corpsmen and MTFs are primary sources of individual casualty data. Casualty reporting in the MARFOR is addressed in MCO P3040.42, *Marine Corps Casualty Procedures Manual*, and other local guidance in the 3040 series. The system described in these directives is essentially one in which personnel losses, regardless of cause, are reported through the chain of command to a central location. Figure 10-1 illustrates the flow of casualty information from medical personnel and MTFs upward through the chain of command.

10001. Field Medical Card

Hospital corpsmen at the unit level usually provide the first written information on a casualty through the use of a U.S. Field Medical Card (DD Form 1380). The field medical card (FMC) is a casualty tag printed in a set which provides a tough original copy for attaching to the casualty (whether wounded or deceased). A carbon copy is retained by the hospital corpsman rendering initial treatment.

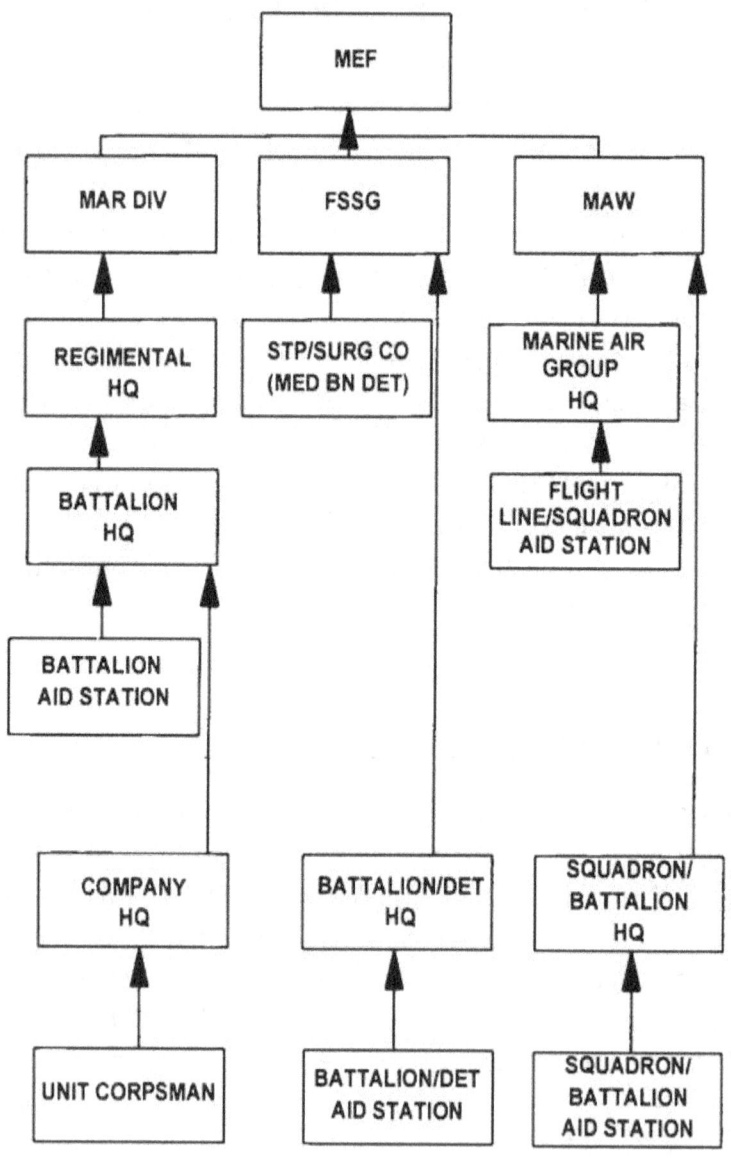

Figure 10-1. Combat Casualty Reporting in the Marine

Expeditionary Force.

The purpose of the FMC is to establish patient accountability and to provide a means to document assessment of condition and treatment rendered by HSS personnel. The FMC is used as an emergency medical tag for all casualties at the time they are initially treated in the field or field medical facility. The completed FMC is an important medical record that will accompany the casualty through the continuum of care. It is also an administrative document that may contain the most dependable information a commanding officer may have regarding a casualty in his unit. Our North Atlantic Treaty Organization allies, by formal agreement, use FMCs containing the same essential information as recorded on the U.S. card.

10002. Identification Tags

Identification tags (dog tags) are essential to casualty identification and recording. Each Service member is issued a chain and two tags to be worn at all times. Tags contain the member's name, social security number, blood type, Service component, religious preference, and protective mask size. The member and the unit are both responsible for ensuring that all information is current and accurate. See BUMED Instruction 6150.35, *Medical Warning Tags*, for more information.

Both identification tags remain with a casualty at all times, except when remains are buried in the combat area. One tag is attached to the grave marker, and the other tag stays with the deceased. Joint Pub 4-06, *Joint Tactics, Techniques, and Proce-*

dures for Mortuary Affairs in Joint Operations, provides detailed procedures for handling deceased personnel.

10003. Automated Medical Record Technology

New automated systems will play a significant role across the range of medical operations. One such device is the portable information carrier (PIC) that stores personal information about its owner. The PIC is a hand-carried, abridged electronic medical record which will serve as the primary repository of individual readiness data such as deployability status, casualty prevention training, medical history, and demographic information. This technology will give the care provider electronic read/write capability to record care given to the patient. This technology will enhance combat casualty care and patient tracking capability by interfacing with command and control systems being developed to track patients' movement, assess logistics requirements, and manage medical surveillance.

Chapter 11

Training

The primary goal of all military training is to achieve and maintain the highest level of preparation possible, thereby developing confidence among the troops and ensuring a high state of readiness. The importance of training as a means of enhancing combat readiness is equally important to HSS personnel. This is especially true given the greatly reduced peacetime staffing of HSS units and the difficulty of obtaining realistic, hands-on trauma training.

Reaching this essential state of readiness requires the medical department to contend with unique circumstances and conditions, including manning levels and the coordinated availability of training. In peacetime, the majority of operating forces' units are manned at slightly more than two-thirds of their mobilization strength, while HSS units are generally manned only with half of the personnel required to carry out their wartime mission. Authorized manning levels fill only about 10 percent of medical corps and nurse corps billets within medical battalions. The end result is that upon mobilization more than half of the medical personnel assigned to operating forces HSS units will be augmentees with greatly varying degrees of field medical skills and experience.

11001. Health Service Support Goals

These manning and training capability constraints require that training efforts be directed toward developing a nucleus of personnel highly skilled in the techniques of establishing and effectively operating HSS facilities in the field. This nucleus, when mobilized, becomes the core of each field medical unit and faces the formidable task of receiving large numbers of augmentees and shaping them into effective health delivery teams. It is not possible to lay out a training program which would be applicable to all HSSEs due to geographic, climatic, and mission variation. Individual commanders of HSS units and other key medical department personnel must structure training in light of achievable goals and limiting factors.

Increased Individual Readiness

Efforts to increase and maintain readiness should extend beyond currently assigned personnel and incorporate augmentees into all training evolutions to the maximum degree funds and scheduling will permit. Surgeons and other key personnel should encourage commanders to involve identified augmentation personnel in exercises when possible. In addition to enhancing individual training, this practice will aid in fostering a sense of unit identity and cohesiveness.

Standardized Methods and Procedures

This is a necessary goal which is elevated to paramount importance because it must be done before mobilization. Augmentees must be familiar with and able to depend on well-developed standing operating procedures in the form of desktop procedures and procedural manuals. The importance of this goal cannot be overly stressed.

Increased Operational Effectiveness Through Higher Levels of Individual and Collective Experience

HSS is basic to all operations. Medical department personnel must, to the maximum degree possible, be involved in all phases of every exercise. The necessity of this involvement is easily and often overlooked in peacetime due to budgetary and time constraints.

11002. Training Pipeline

The following training courses are essential to the development of effective, efficient, and successful HSS personnel. Course quota management and control are under the cognizance of BUMED.

Field Medical Service School

There are two Field Medical Service Schools (FMSSs), one at Camp Lejeune, North Carolina, and the other at Camp Pendleton, California. The mission of these Marine Corps schools is to prepare Navy medical department personnel for service with the MARFOR. Before reporting to the MARFOR, all medical department personnel (officer and enlisted) not having previous field medical service training shall attend an appropriate course of instruction at one of the schools. Both schools teach—

• The role and requirements of HSS units in the field.

• Military tactical and defensive techniques closely related to field HSS.

- HSS planning and concepts for officers and senior petty officers, including medical estimates, medical staff planning, and logistics support.

- MARFOR and MAGTF organization.

- The use and handling of designated table of organization weapons for medical department personnel.

Combat Casualty Care Course

Before reporting to the MARFOR, all medical department officers who are clinical providers (i.e., medical corps, dental corps, nurse corps) shall attend a course of instruction in advanced combat life support. In combat support operations, nonphysician health care providers may be required to assist medical officers in presurgical preparation and wound management. Training is available through the Defense Medical Readiness Training Institute, Fort Sam Houston, Texas.

11003. Commander's Responsibilities

Commander's are responsible for ensuring that all command personnel receive appropriate training in both military and technical subject areas, including emergency medical training of nonmedical personnel and the continued training of medical department personnel in field medical practices and related military subjects. Commanders develop, conduct, and evaluate individual and collective HSS training based on training standards published by the Marine Corps Combat Development Command (MCCDC). When standards have not been published, unit commanders ensure training is based on this MCWP and other doctrinal, tactical, and technical publications approved for Navy and Marine Corps use.

11004. Medical Department Officers and Senior Enlisted

The division and wing surgeons maintain staff supervision of all medical training programs, including exercise planning and execution, for medical department personnel assigned to their respective subordinate commands. Within the FSSG, the group surgeon and dental officer, in coordination with the G-3, exercises staff cognizance of all general medical training programs. Medical and dental battalion commanders are responsible for all battalion training programs including internal planning and execution. The FSSG HSSO exercises staff cognizance of FSSG planning and exercises. All medical department officers and senior hospital and dental corps conduct and/or supervise the training of hospital corpsmen and dental technicians.

11005. Types of Training

Individual Training

Individual training may be conducted in a formal school or at the member's command. This training prepares an individual to perform specific tasks related to general military duties or assigned specialties. Medical department personnel who regularly perform duties of their occupational specialty develop increased confidence and proficiency. Individual training may include first aid and cardiopulmonary resuscitation (CPR) as well as more formal programs such as the Plans, Operations, and Medical Intelligence Course; the Joint Medical Planners Course; the Landing Force Medical Staff Planning Course; and the Medical Regulating Course.

Unit Training

Unit training prepares an individual to function within a unit and as part of a cohesive element. Such elements may include teams, platoons, sections, companies, or whatever size is feasible. MARFOR unit training is normally conducted afloat or in a field environment and involves the entire organization, including assigned HSSEs. Unit training has proven most effective when conducted in a simulated combat environment. These exercises entail setting up treatment facilities in the field and treatment of simulated casualties. Other field units such as infantry battalions, regiments, and combat support and combat service support organizations conduct field training exercises that involve HSS personnel organic to those units.

Exercises

Training exercises provide a realistic training environment, allowing HSS personnel to apply and refine their field medical skills as well as expand their knowledge and skills in the following areas:

- LF organization and communications.
- HSS functions in the field.
- Deployment procedures, including combat loading of HSS equipment.
- Sanitation standards for shipboard and field troops.

- Ship-to-shore operations.
- Casualty evacuation.
- Mass casualty training.
- HSS supply and resupply.
- Operations in severe environments.
- Special problems in the amphibious objective area.

Nuclear, Biological, and Chemical Training

Readiness training for patient decontamination, patient care, and NBC defense may be conducted at individual or unit level. Training in medical procedures associated with NBC casualties cannot be adequately addressed in on-the-job training but requires the participation of instructors specifically trained in the subject area. (See FMFM 11-11, *Treatment of Chemical Agent Casualties and Conventional Military Chemical Injuries.*)

Preventive Medicine Training

HSS personnel in all MARFOR units must receive instruction in the recognition of diseases and environmental hazards that may occur within a specific area of operations. Emphasis should be placed on personal and unit-wide preventive medicine measures at all levels. Division, group, and wing surgeons should periodically review contingency plans, with emphasis on identifying measures necessary to effectively prevent disease and other health hazards. This information should be incorporated into training programs for medical department personnel.

Logistics and Supply Training

The Marine Corps and Navy supply systems are sufficiently different to invalidate most information in Navy training manuals with regard to its applicability to the Marine Corps system. Unit commanders with a health care mission must ensure Navy personnel are sufficiently trained in basic procedures to operate within the Marine Corps supply system.

11006. Dental Personnel

Enlisted dental personnel assigned to the MARFOR receive the same basic FMSS training as hospital corpsmen, but rate specific training for their individual Navy enlisted classification codes. During casualty overload, dental personnel perform roles in combat casualty care. Training emphasis should be placed on increasing skills in combat casualty care and trauma management, including training in the designated roles of preoperative preparation and wound management for dental officers and ward corpsmen duties and central sterilization duties for dental technicians.

11007. Non-Health Service Support Personnel

HSS personnel are responsible for training non-HSS personnel in subjects such as CPR, first aid, buddy aid, personal hygiene, field sanitation, and preventive medicine.

All non-HSS personnel (including chaplains and religious programs enlisted personnel) should receive extensive training in first aid procedures, self-aid, buddy aid, and personal decontamination. Field Manual (FM) 21-11, *First Aid for Soldiers*, and the Marine Corps Institute's *Marine Battle Skills Training Handbook* series list and explain subjects that must be taught.

Personnel should be indoctrinated in specific personal protection and disease prevention topics as described in FM 21-10, *Field Hygiene and Sanitation*, and NAVMED P-5010.

Marine Corps supply personnel in key positions shall be provided training in procedures that enable them to provide medical supply support when deployed. Training should encompass interfacing with the SIMLM system.

Further information on the availability and applicability of specific individual or unit HSS training can be found by addressing Director, Training and Education Division, MCCDC, or Director, Operational Readiness and Training Division, BUMED.

(reverse blank)

Appendix A

Blood Support

Formally established as the Military Blood Program in 1952 by Presidential Order as part of the National Blood Program, today's Armed Services Blood Program (ASBP) consists of approximately 116 blood banks and blood donor centers worldwide, including 43 Food and Drug Administration (FDA) licensed blood donor centers. The ASBP mission is to provide quality blood products, blood substitutes, and services for all worldwide customers in peace and war. The ASBP is a joint program operated by the military Services and coordinated by the Armed Services Blood Program Office (ASBPO).

The ASBPO is a joint health agency charted to monitor the implementation of blood program policies established by the Assistant Secretary of Defense (Health Affairs) (ASD[HA]) and to coordinate the blood programs of the military Services (Army, Air Force, and Navy) and the unified commands as directed in DOD Instruction 6480.4, *Armed Services Blood Program Operational Procedures*. The ASBPO provides standardization among the Services and enhances the total blood distribution system in peace and war. The U.S. Army Surgeon General, on behalf of the Secretary of the Army, serves as the executive agent for the ASBPO for administrative support and staff supervision. The Joint Chiefs of Staff, by Memorandum of Understanding, are responsible for the review and provision of guidance in all matters regarding blood support in joint operational planning. The ASD(HA) provides policy guidance to the ASBPO. All of the ASBP elements function together to successfully operate the Military Blood Program.

Blood support for the MARFOR is provided by the Navy's Blood Program (NBP). The NBP ensures operational readiness to both the Navy and MARFOR through a viable blood program which meets and exceeds standards of practice. The NBP oversees 30 Navy blood banks worldwide. Of those 30, 19 are with blood donor centers (BDCs). The NBP operates under the FDA License Number 635. The responsible head is the Surgeon General of the Navy/Chief, Bureau of Medicine and Surgery. The alternate responsible head is the Assistant Chief for Operational Medicine and Fleet Support, Bureau of Medicine and Surgery.

Armed Services Whole Blood Processing Laboratory

An Armed Services Whole Blood Processing Laboratory (ASWBPL) is a USAF-managed, tri-service-staffed, central repository for liquid and frozen blood required in peacetime, contingencies, and war. An ASWBPL releases blood to unified commands upon approval by the ASBPO. Theater MTFs may not go directly to the ASWBPL for blood. ASWBPLs—

* Retype blood for A, B, and O blood types and Rh only.

* Pack, ice, and prepare blood for shipment to the theater.

* Maintain a peacetime inventory of 250 units of liquid blood for use as a rapid response requirement.

Joint Blood Program Office

The Joint Blood Program Office (JBPO) is responsible for the joint blood program management in a theater of operations. The

JBPO functions as part of the unified command surgeon's office but may establish an Area Joint Blood Program Office (AJBPO) for regional blood management. The JBPO—

- Works directly for the unified command surgeon. The JBPO may augment the surgeon's staff of the Commander, Joint Task Force.

- Serves as the central point of contact to ASBPO.

- Coordinates joint blood products requirements and capabilities in the theater of operations. Major assessment areas for a JBPO are manpower, training levels, and supplies.

- Coordinates requirements, distribution, and facilities. The JBPO ensures blood is where it's needed. The JBPO quickly determines how to get blood to forward units and Navy ships as well as MTFs.

- Monitors shortfalls within the unified command, including supplies for collection, deglycerolization, distribution, and transfusion of blood/blood products.

- Ensures readiness by having a distribution system, exercises, and training. Other theater staff members (AJBPO, blood support unit [BSU], and MTF officers) may need further training on coordinating with medical planners or transportation officers to anticipate blood/supply needs, making transportation arrangements, or using liquid/frozen products.

- Ensures compliance with ASBP policies, FDA regulations, American Association of Blood Banks standards in peacetime, contingencies, and war.

- Serves as the unified command subject matter expert on determining blood requirements based on Joint Staff casualty projections and maintaining blood in medical sustainment analysis.

- Provides the joint blood concept; coordinates with logistics, transportation, and communications personnel on the Joint Staff for the unified command; and prepares appendix 2 to Annex Q, *Planning Guidance, Medical Services.*

Area Joint Blood Program Office

AJBPOs can be established within the theater of operations during war or special operations. An AJBPO coordinates requirements and distribution of blood products to support BSUs and MTFs in a specific area, regardless of the Service component. Not all operations will require establishing an AJBPO. An AJBPO may not be a blood bank specialist but will have most of the same responsibilities as the JBPO and may need training and additional guidance from the JBPO.

Blood Transshipment Centers

A blood transshipment center (BTC) is the central receiving point for blood shipments from the ASWBPL and for issue to the BSUs. A BTC can store and process up to 7,200 units of liquid blood daily. A BTC is usually staffed and operated by USAF personnel at a major airhead. BTC blood products are managed by the JBPO or AJBPO (if established). One or more BTCs may be located in each theater of operation. Not all theaters of operations will require the use of a BTC. BTCs—

- Inspect blood received from the ASWBPL or other blood agencies, blood products depots, or other BTCs.

- Store, ice, and re-ice blood and perform quality control.

- Issue blood to BSUs or other component blood users.

- Prepare daily blood reports for JBPO and blood shipment reports for receiving BSU.

Transportable Blood Transshipment Centers

Transportable Blood Transshipment Centers (TBTCs) are mobile, modular, and can be transported into the theater of operations at a site designated by the theater commander. Although TBTCs have the capacity to store frozen blood products, they can deploy with or without those products. Based on theater commanders decisions, the ASBP will have six TBTCs available as blood program elements and one for training deployable personnel.

Blood Products Depots

Blood products depots (BPDs) are located within the unified command to maintain large quantities of frozen blood products for use during armed conflicts or emergencies requiring medical support. These prepositioned stocks of frozen blood products are intended to fulfill initial wartime blood surge requirements until mobilization of CONUS assets can catch up to demand. Subsequent liquid blood supplies will come from CONUS blood donor centers and will be shipped via the ASWBPL and the BTCs.

BPDs are single Service staffed and operated, but the blood products are for use by all components in potential theaters of conflict. Blood maintained at BPDs is managed by the JBPO via the

AJBPO. Not all unified commands and theaters of operations will require or have a BPD. BPDs—

• Store frozen blood products until required.

• Issue blood as directed by the JBPO via the AJBPO.

• Thaw and deglycerolize frozen red cells and distribute to BSUs.

Blood Supply Units

Blood supply units (BSUs) receive, store, and distribute blood within the theater of operations. BSUs are required to provide a 5-day storage supply of blood products based on MTF proposed requirements and blood reports.

BSUs can provide support in a specific geographical area regardless of Service components and can support up to 12 MTFs designated by the JBPO.

The following units/facilities can serve as a BSU: Army blood platoon, Navy fleet hospital, naval amphibious assault vessels, T-AH hospital ships, MTFs, and BPD, when designated.

BSUs provide storage capabilities that maintain temperature requirements for liquid blood.

BSUs can produce ice for shipping and re-icing of blood in the theater. They can also store frozen blood products, including fresh frozen plasma and frozen red cells. A BSU's ability to obtain and store dry ice provides the means to ship fresh frozen plasma to MTFs.

BSUs can collect blood in emergencies, but this is not encouraged due to the lack of capability to perform testing for infectious diseases. Refer to the emergency donor section for protocol regarding blood drawn in theater.

BSUs can support MTFs as designated/determined by the JBPO.

(reverse blank)

Appendix B

Authorized Medical and Dental Allowance Lists

HSS authorized medical allowance lists (AMALs) and author-ized dental allowance lists (ADALs) are configured in assem-blages such as equipment and supply. The equipment assemblage contains equipment and reusable materiel required to establish the basic function of the assemblage (e.g., an operating room). The supply assemblage contains consumable material to support the function in treating a designated number of casualties or to perform a specific task. For readiness purposes, an equipment module may be stored in combination with its corresponding supply module. The materiel listed in each AMAL/ADAL is the minimum amount to be maintained.

Marine Corps Order 4400 series contains AMAL and ADAL procurement policies and procedures. Policies and procedures include assembly, maintenance, levels of supply, and distribution of materiel. AMALs and ADALs are maintained and resupplied by the medical logistics company, supply battalion, FSSG.

Numbers and Nomenclatures

AMAL 618—Laboratory Equipment. Equipment and reusable materiel required to establish a laboratory capable of hematol-ogy, microbiology, urinalysis, and chemical testing.

AMAL 619—Laboratory Supply. Consumable supplies required to perform hematology, microbiology, urinalysis, and chemical testing for 100 patients.

AMAL 627—X-ray Equipment. Equipment and reusable materiel required to establish one x-ray room and processing facility.

AMAL 649—X-ray Supply. Consumable supplies required to provide x-ray support for 100 patients at 10 films per patient.

AMAL 629—Pharmacy Equipment. Equipment and reusable materiel required to establish a pharmacy.

AMAL 630—Pharmacy Supply. Consumable supplies required to provide pharmacy support for 1,000 patients in six 5-day packages for a total of 30 days.

AMAL 631—Shock Surgical Team/Triage Equipment. Equipment and reusable materiel required to establish a basic shock trauma surgical team or triage to receive, resuscitate, sort, and temporarily hold casualties.

AMAL 632—Shock Surgical Team/Triage Supply. Consumable supplies required to receive, resuscitate, sort, and temporarily hold 50 casualties with major wounds and to provide basic line corpsman resupply.

AMAL 633—Ward Equipment. Equipment and reusable materiel required to establish a 20-bed unit.

AMAL 634—Ward Supply. Consumable supplies required to provide ward support for 100 bed days-to-patient.

AMAL 635—Aid Station Equipment. Equipment and reusable materiel required to support one division, wing, group, engineer, or battalion aid station.

AMAL 636—Aid Station Supply. Consumable supplies required to provide aid station support, initial resuscitation, and stabilization of 50 casualties with major wounds prior to evacuation, and to resupply basic line corpsman.

AMAL 637—Preventive Medicine Equipment. Equipment and reusable materiel required to establish a preventive medicine section. The section provides technical preventive medicine advice; inspects food service operations, waste disposal, water potability and sources, and vector control; coordinates control measures required for communicable diseases; and monitors and assists immunization programs.

AMAL 638—Preventive Medicine Supply. Consumable supplies required to provide support of the preventive medicine effort to the MEF in twelve 5-day packages for a total of 60 days.

AMAL 639—Operating Room Equipment. Equipment and reusable materiel required to support an operating room for performing major surgical procedures, administering general anesthesia, sterilizing materiel, and maintaining sterile material.

AMAL 640—Operating Room Supply. Consumable supplies required to provide operating room support for 25 surgical cases.

ADAL 662—Field Dental Operatory. Equipment and reusable materiel required to establish a dental clinic in the field. Consumable supplies required to provide emergency, diagnostic, and preventive maintenance dental care for 400 patients.

AMAL 684—Geographic Supplement. Consumable supplies and reusable materiel required to accommodate special mission- and geographic-related requirements for a MEF in twelve 5-day packages for a total of 60 days.

AMAL 685—Cold Weather Supplement. Consumable supplies and reusable materiel required to accommodate special mission- and geographic-related requirements in areas where cold-related injuries are likely to occur.

AMAL 686—Hot Weather Supplement. Consumable supplies and reusable materiel required to accommodate special mission- and geographic-related requirements into areas where heat-related injuries are likely to occur.

AMAL 687—NBC Individual. Materials required for the individual to conduct primary decontamination and treatment in an NBC environment.

AMAL 688—NBC Unit. Materials required for the units to conduct primary and secondary decontamination and treatment in an NBC environment.

AMAL 691—Med Log Test/Repair Equipment. Equipment and reusable materiel required to perform testing, calibration, and 3d and 4th echelon maintenance of medical/dental equipment.

AMAL 692—Med Log Test/Repair Supply. Consumable supplies required to accommodate a medical repair section in the testing, calibration, and 3d and 4th echelon maintenance of medical/dental equipment.

(reverse blank)

Appendix C

Glossary

ACE	aviation combat element
ADAL	authorized dental allowance lists
AE	aeromedical evacuation
AFMIC	Armed Forces Medical Intelligence Center
AJBPO	Area Joint Blood Program Office
AMAL	authorized medical allowance lists
ASBP	Armed Services Blood Program
ASBPO	Armed Services Blood Program Office
ASD (HA)	Assistant Secretary of Defense (Health Affairs)
ASWBPL	Armed Services Whole Blood Processing Laboratory
ATF	amphibious task force
BAS	battalion aid station
BDC	blood donor centers
BPD	Blood Products Depots
BSSG	brigade service support group
BSU	blood support unit
BTC	blood transshipment center
BUMED	U.S. Navy Bureau of Medicine and Surgery
CATF	commander, amphibious task force
CINC	commander in chief
CJCSM	Chairman of the Joint Chiefs of Staff Manual
CLF	commander, landing force
COMDTPUB	Commandant Publication (U.S. Coast Guard)
CONPLAN	concept plan
CONUS	continental United States

CPR .... cardiopulmonary resuscitation
CRTS .... casualty receiving and treatment ship
CSSE .... combat service support element
CSSOC .... combat service support operations center

DOD .... Department of Defense
FDA
Food and Drug Administration
FLAS .... flight line aid station
FM .... U.S. Army field manual
FMC .... field medical card
FMFM .... Fleet Marine Force manual
FMSS .... Field Medical Service School
FSSG .... force service support group
FST .... fleet surgical team

GCCS .... Global Command and Control System
GCE .... ground combat element
GCSS .... Global Combat Support System

H&S .... headquarters and service
HSS .... health service support
HSSD .... health service support detachment
HSSE .... health service support element
HSSO .... health service support officer

JBPO .... Joint Blood Program Office

LAN .... local area network
LF .... landing force
LFSP .... landing force support party
LHA .... amphibious assault ship (general purpose)

LHD ....amphibious assault ship (multipurpose)
LMCC .... logistics movement coordination center
LPH................................amphibious assault ship (helicopter)

MAG .... Marine aircraft group
MAGTF .... Marine air-ground task force
MAP...Medical Augmentation Program
MARFOR...Marine Corps forces
MAW .... Marine aircraft wing
MCCDC ....Marine Corps Combat Development Command
MCO ....Marine Corps order
MCPP.. Marine Corps planning process
MCWP ....Marine Corps warfighting publication
Med Log Co ....medical logistics company
MEF ....Marine expeditionary force
METT-T ....mission, enemy, terrain and weather, troops
                                    and support available-time available
MEU...Marine expeditionary unit
MMART .... mobile medical augmentation readiness team
MOPP.....................................mission-oriented protective posture
MSSG...MEU service support group
MTF .... medical treatment facility
MWSS.. Marine wing support squadron

NAVMED.. naval medical
NBC ....nuclear, biological, and chemical
NBP.. Navy Blood Program
NWP..naval warfare publication

OPLAN ....operation plan
OPORD .... operation order

PIC .... portable information carrier
PMI .... primary movement items

SHF .... super high frequency
SIMLM .... single integrated medical logistics manager
STP .... shock trauma platoon
Surg Co .... surgical company

TBTC .... Transportable Blood Transshipment Center
T/E .... table of equipment
TMIP .... theater medical information program
TTP .... tactics, techniques, and procedures

USAF .... United States Air Force
USMC .... United States Marine Corps

VHF .... very high frequency

WAN .... wide area network

Appendix D

References and Related Publications

Chairman of the Joint Chiefs of Staff Manual (CJCSM)

3122.03   Joint Operation Planning and Execution System
               Volume II, Planning Formats and Guidance

Joint Publications

4-02   Doctrine for Health Service Support in Joint
               Operations
4-02.2   Joint Tactics, Techniques, and Procedures for
               Patient Movement in Joint Operations
4-06   Joint Tactics, Techniques, and Procedures for
               Mortuary Affairs in Joint Operations

Department of Defense (DOD) Instruction

6480.4   Armed Services Blood Program Operational
               Procedures

Navy Publications

Navy Warfare Publications (NWPs)

1-14M   Commander's Handbook of the Law of Naval
               Operations
4-02   Operational Health Service Support

| 4-02.2 | Patient Movement |
| 4-02.4 | Part A Deployable Health Service Support Platforms—Fleet Hospitals |

NAVMED

| P 5010 | BUMED Manual of Naval Preventive Medicine |

Bureau of Medicine and Surgery (BUMED) Instruction

| 6150.35 | Medical Warning Tags |

COMDTPUB

| P5800.7 | The Commander's Handbook on the Law of Naval Operations |

Marine Corps Publications

Marine Corps Doctrinal Publication (MCDP)

| 2 | Intelligence |

Marine Corps Warfighting Publication (MCWP)

| 2-3 | Intelligence Analysis and Production (under development) |
| 5-2.1 | The Commander's Handbook on the Law of Naval Operations |

Fleet Marine Force Manuals (FMFMs)

0-25	The Law of Land Warfare
4-50	Health Service Support
5-30	Assault Support
11-11	Treatment of Chemical Agent Casualties and Conventional Military Chemical Injuries

Fleet Marine Force Reference Publication (FMFRP)

1-18	Amphibious Ships and Landing Craft Data Book

Marine Corps Handbooks

Marine Battle Skills Training Handbook

Marine Corps Orders (MCOs)

P3040.42	Marine Corps Casualty Procedures Manual
4400	Series Supply/Materiel

Army Publications

Field Manuals (FMs)

21-10	Field Hygiene and Sanitation
21-11	First Aid for Soldiers
27-10	The Law of Land Warfare

Department of the Army Pamphlet (DA PAM)

27-1	Treaties Governing Land Warfare

(reverse blank)

www.ingramcontent.com/pod-product-compliance
Lightning Source LLC
Chambersburg PA
CBHW070749290526
45795CB00002B/533

* 9 781491 033395 *